Piano · Vocal · Guitar

# SARAH MCLACHLAN
## LAWS OF ILLUSION

ISBN 978-1-4234-9868-1

7777 W. BLUEMOUND RD. P.O. BOX 13819 MILWAUKEE, WI 53213

D0584875

Visit Hal Leonard Online at
**www.halleonard.com**

# CONTENTS

# AWAKENINGS

Words and Music by
SARAH McLACHLAN

# ILLUSIONS OF BLISS

Words and Music by SARAH McLACHLAN
and PIERRE MARCHAND

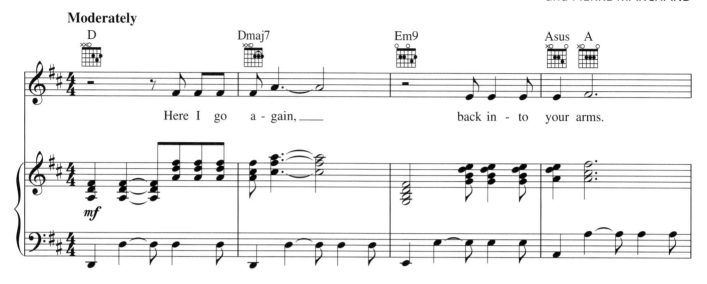

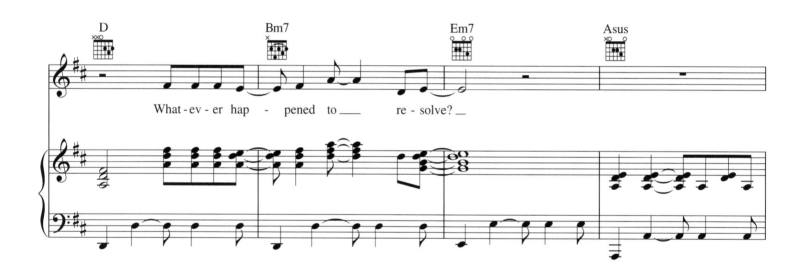

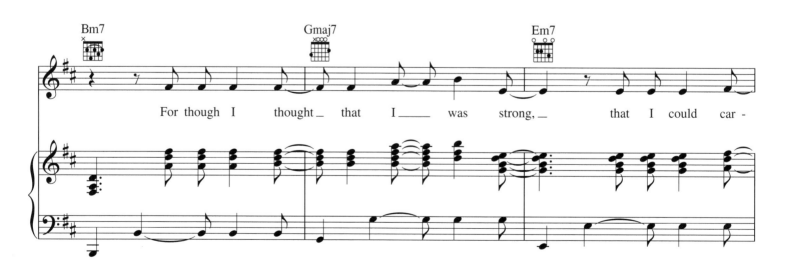

# LOVING YOU IS EASY

Words and Music by
SARAH McLACHLAN

Lov - ing you is _____ eas - y, _____ lov - ing you is

won - drous _____ and pure. _____ I shout it from the roof - tops. How long _____

_____ must I wait 'til I _____ see your smile? Might have been the

# CHANGES

Words and Music by SARAH McLACHLAN
and PIERRE MARCHAND

CODA

New walls, new lad-ders,

# FORGIVENESS

Words and Music by
SARAH McLACHLAN

**Moderate Ballad**

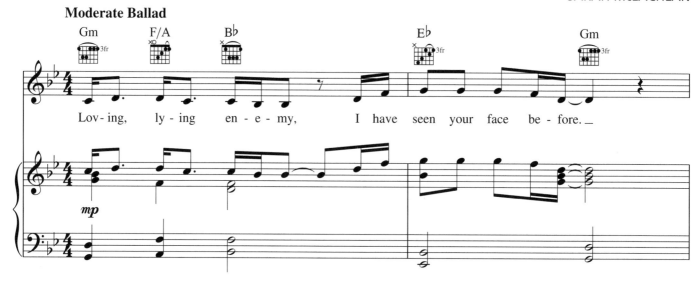

Lov-ing, ly-ing en-e-my, I have seen your face be-fore. __

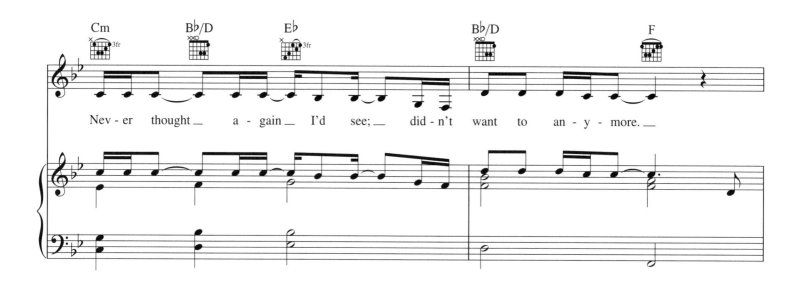

Nev-er thought __ a-gain __ I'd see; __ did-n't want to an-y-more. __

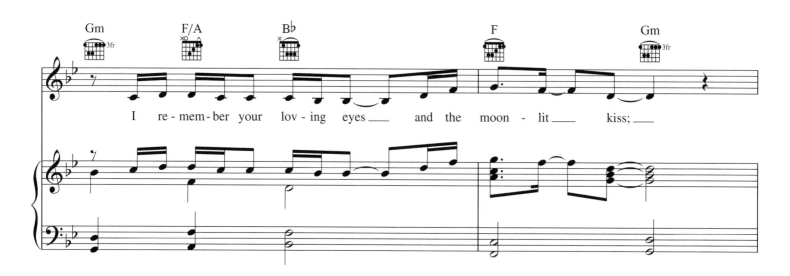

I re-mem-ber your lov-ing eyes __ and the moon-lit __ kiss; __

# RIVERS OF LOVE

Words and Music by SARAH McLACHLAN
and PIERRE MARCHAND

long have you wait- ed, how long _____ 'til you drown? __

# LOVE COME

Words and Music by
SARAH McLACHLAN

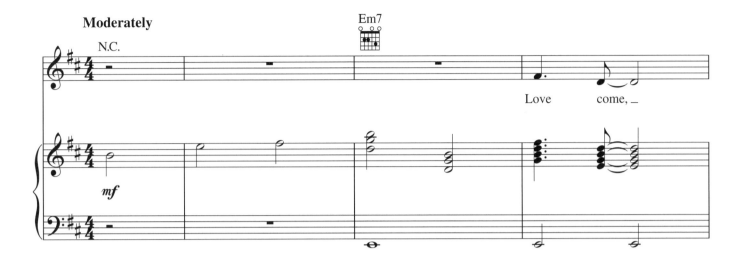

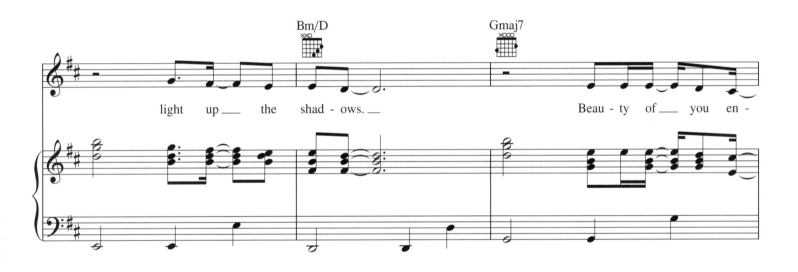

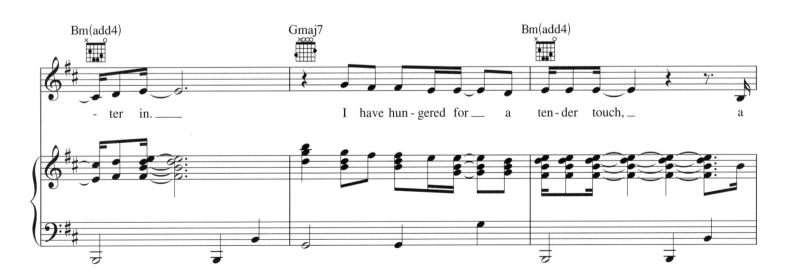

long and lone- ly time. _____

Oo,

oh. _____

Oo. _____

# OUT OF TUNE

Words and Music by SARAH McLACHLAN
and PIERRE MARCHAND

# HEARTBREAK

Words and Music by SARAH McLACHLAN
and PIERRE MARCHAND

**Moderate Rock beat**

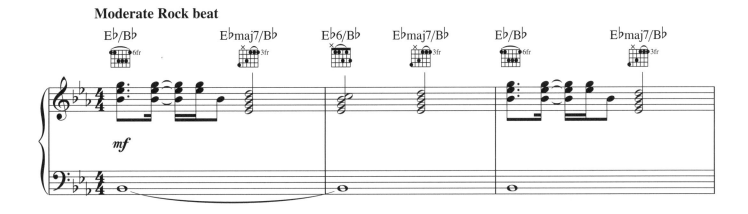

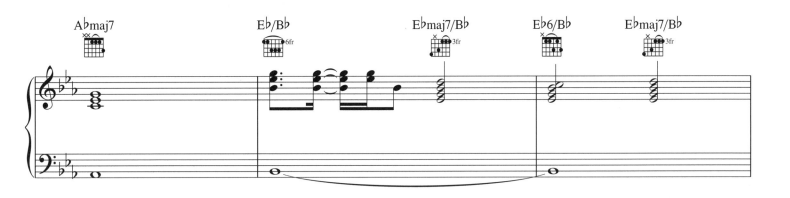

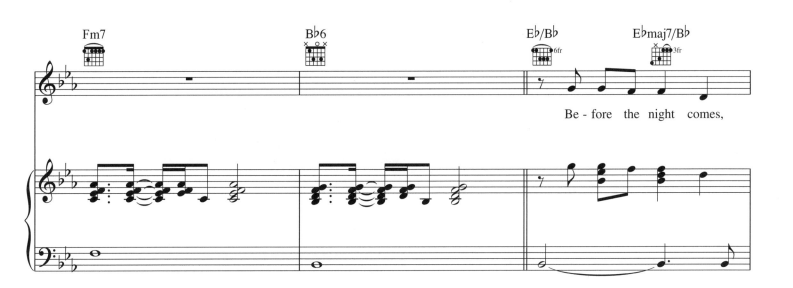

Be - fore the night comes,

64

# DON'T GIVE UP ON US

Words and Music by SARAH McLACHLAN
and PIERRE MARCHAND

Moderately, with a shuffle

Love has \_\_ tak-en me for a fool, \_\_

got-ten out in time \_\_ to save him-self, \_\_\_ mmm. \_\_

Should have known \_\_ bet-ter \_\_ but I \_\_\_ let things slide. \_\_ I

# U WANT ME 2

Words and Music by SARAH McLACHLAN
and PIERRE MARCHAND

*Recorded a half step lower.*

# BRING ON THE WONDER

Words and Music by
SUSAN ENAN